Fifty Classic Piano Rags

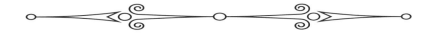

with an Introduction by
Rudi Blesh

Dover Publications, Inc.
Mineola, New York

Bibliographical Note

Fifty Classic Piano Rags, first published in 2010 by Dover Publications, Inc., is a new selection of music from *Classic Piano Rags*, published by Dover Publications, Inc., in 1973. The original publishers and dates of publication of the music appear on the individual title pages. The Introduction was specially prepared for the 1973 edition.

International Standard Book Number

ISBN-13: 978-0-486-47397-0
ISBN-10: 0-486-47397-X

Manufactured in the United States by Courier Corporation
47397X01
www.doverpublications.com

Introduction

This decade of the 1970's seems to be on its way to becoming the era of the rediscovery of America. We rediscover the green land and the last disappearing patches of wilderness; we rediscover our waters—rivers, lakes, sea—and our maltreated air—the once-blue sky—and all the harried, hunted creatures—furred, feathered, scaled. We are the long-absent ones, our homecoming one of delight and of fear in more or less equal amounts. For only too evidently our rediscovery may be just in time.

If our very land and air could have been, essentially, all but lost, it should not be surprising that for more than half a century we forgot our most charming and most American classical music: ragtime.

So, after the long reign of the jazz trumpets and in the very midst of the roar of Rock's amplified guitars, we are finding all kinds of earlier American music: Gottschalk, Sousa, Billings, Ives. But, especially, we are rediscovering that syncopated, tonal art nouveau jewelry called (as if Mark Twain had named it) "ragtime," that syncopated fin-de-siècle keyboard music that once flowed as pure as did our rivers. We are rediscovering native genius, Black and White, in the homespun rural artist Charles Hunter; in Percy Wenrich, the small-town boy atingle with talent; as well as in Thomas Million Turpin, the classic pioneer; and in the classic giants, the "Bach-Beethoven-Brahms" of ragtime, Scott Joplin, James Sylvester Scott and Joseph Francis Lamb.

And, with something like awe, we are glimpsing at last how this gentle music almost literally exploded, going from the country banjos to Joplin's twilight classic, *Reflection,* in less than four decades, while the creative span from Bach to Brahms covered two centuries!

The time it took for our rediscovery is another matter. We set no startling record in this respect. It took the world about 100 years (1750 to 1850) to rediscover Bach (with the valiant efforts of an enlightened few, led by Mendelssohn). With all our vaunted speed by land and by air, it has still taken us over half a century to recognize our ragtime heritage for what it is.

However long it took, ragtime is a rich and rewarding find. It was the first native music thoroughly to encompass the contradictory American spirit—lively yet romantic, sanguine yet pensive, energized yet tender, adventurous yet irenic—a spirit as resistant to explanation as it is palpable and unmistakable when perfectly expressed. Ragtime was the first native music to include in creation and performance both of the races, Black and White. Ragtime, too, like America itself was both like and unlike Europe, with Continental qualities and their antitheses. Strangest of all, it issued in its origins from no Caucasian majority but from the deprived American minority of dark-skinned people. And it came from no conservatories nor, even, from studios however humble. It bloomed in the lurid nights of those inner cities of the 90's, the infamous red-light districts of brothels, saloons, casinos and wine rooms.

Today, with pornography everywhere, the tenderloin milieu of ragtime development might be construed as one of the prime reasons for its current rediscovery and new acceptance. But this would be a sad error to make, even if ragtime had in truth been soiled by its youthful associations. To the contrary: Scott Joplin's justly famous *Maple Leaf Rag* is an affirmation not of blatant sexuality but of a pure, triumphant musicality. And, for exhibit, there is a far simpler little rag of the same period: Jelly Roll Morton of New Orleans played it in a Storyville brothel to accompany the girls' stripping for the out-of-town buyers. Yet it is a tune of such innocence that it survived to serve, unbeknownst to all, as the musical theme for the children's television show, *Kukla, Fran, and Ollie,* without acknowledgment of its real title, *The Naked Dance!*

Our rediscovery of ragtime needs, indeed, to include the facts that answer the question: why were the creators of ragtime in the bawdy houses and honky-tonks to begin with? The answer is simple and damning, to us and not to them: they were Black, with a few disowned Whites, and this was the only place they could find work. Briefly, we exiled the ragtimers there and then shunned them for being there.

So it came about that ragtime's enforced milieu was the cause of a bitter battle between prejudice and acceptance even during the very heyday of its popular acceptance. Now, three-quarters of a century later, in our day of Eros this milieu should scarcely motivate the acceptance of ragtime any more than it would the acceptance of Toulouse-Lautrec's memorabilia of the *maisons de tolérance.*

To grasp the brutal irony implicit in the flowering of the classic ragtime, perhaps one should try to imagine the young Mozart playing and composing in bagnios rather than at the imperial court. One might well wonder: would his music and his genius have survived? Well, that of a teenage Scott Joplin and of some of his creative fellows did. And it was there, during the crucial decade of 1896–1906, that an itinerant, half-illiterate—but utterly charming—country dance music moved from the banjo echoes of plantation and levee to the fully realized classicism of Scott Joplin. The *Maple Leaf Rag, "The Easy Winners," Elite Syncopations, The Entertainer, The Cascades* and the rest, a near-score of masterpieces, would be the precious core of classic ragtime as they are of this present collection.

Joplin was the first true classicist of the piano rag and he was consciously so. He was born in 1868, right after the Civil War, to a poor Black family in the then frontier settlement of Texarkana. His early talent (like that of a Black Mozart) was miraculously fostered by a White classical music teacher. Joplin was a wanderer in his teens, and his peripatetic pianism, cast naturally in the polyrhythmic Afro-American mold later to be called ragtime, was the creative child of a musical intellect both folk-conscious and classically oriented.

Joplin was 31 before his first piano rag, *Original Rags,* achieved publication. The *Maple Leaf Rag* followed the same year and was an immediate, resounding (and long-lived) hit. Suddenly prosperous and free to leave the honky-tonks for the more congenial life of teaching and composing, Joplin, nevertheless, having initially acknowledged in the title the semi-rowdy sporting club where he had composed it, in its second edition (1901) made his gratitude specific in the inscription at the top of the cover: "To the Maple Leaf Club." This is the act—both humble and proud—of a superior person.

Moving on in later years to operatic composition, denied performance, and, finally, dying in the dark midnight of madness in 1917, Joplin is the towering Bach of ragtime: not, of course, in musical spirit or style, but in the crucial importance of his position in the development of the music. It is hard to conceive of a classic ragtime without Joplin—he initiated the concept of classicism and perfected its form. In fairness one should add that in all likelihood even Joplin could not have accomplished this without the early help of White capital in the person of his extraordinary friend, the music publisher John Stillwell Stark.

The scene of classic ragtime was the Missouri Valley area of Missouri and Kansas, with the adjacent fringes of Arkansas, Tennessee, Texas and the Oklahoma and Indian Territories. Its focal points were, successively, Sedalia and St. Louis. In Sedalia, Joplin centered the creative activity and sponsored young talent as he himself had been sponsored. Thus we have the classic rags of the younger Arthur Marshall and Scott Hayden, one by the former a collaboration with Joplin ("*Swipesy*" *Cake Walk*) and his own creations ("*Kinklets,*" *The Peach,* etc.) and those by the latter both Joplin-Hayden collaborations ("*Something Doing*" and *Sun Flower Slow Drag*).

The St. Louis scene, which predated Sedalia, also continued after the Sedalia decline that came when Joplin and his protegés moved to the Mississippi riverfront metropolis. In earlier, pre-Sedalia visits, Joplin had met the St. Louis ragtime coterie, which centered around the redoubtable giant Tom Turpin, saloon-keeper, self-taught composer and pianistic marvel. Turpin's *Harlem Rag,* published two years before the *Maple Leaf,* is the first published Black rag. (The earliest of three versions appears here.)

Moving in 1900 to St. Louis (where he would reside until 1907), Joplin set up a studio and concentrated on teaching and composing. Though he never reentered the red-light world he maintained friendly contact with the now larger rag fraternity at Turpin's Rosebud Cafe and its neighboring private ragtimers' rendezvous, the Hurrah Sporting Club. Among the newer arrivals was Joe Jordan—he would later move to wider musical success in Chicago. His slow drag, *Nappy Lee,* dates from the St. Louis days. Another new enlistee was Artie Matthews, brilliant technician with an equally brilliant musical mind. In 1912 Matthews would publish the first Afro-American blues (*Baby Seals Blues*), slightly predating even the great W. C. Handy. But his reputation rests more on the remarkable series of five rags called the

Pastime Rags. Though the series was composed in St. Louis, their publication occupied John Stark sporadically from 1913 to 1920, long after Matthews had moved to Cincinnati, founded his Cosmopolitan Conservatory of Music and withdrawn from ragtime. The complete *Pastime* series, No. 1 to No. 5, (here published together for the first time), though never popular hits, are a wholly remarkable group. No. 1 with barrelhouse "walking" bass, No. 5 with tango bass and No. 4 with treble "crazy chord" clusters in the first strain—they are all virtuosic, wide-ranging in concept, a five-chapter synopsis of the St. Louis ragtime scene.

Joplin also met there the darkly handsome, solitary wastrel Creole genius, Louis Chauvin, whose incredible fingers tossed off beautiful impromptu rags heard once by heedless ears and never again. When Joplin left St. Louis in 1907 for his *Wanderjahre,* he found Chauvin in Chicago, dying of syphilis. In the haunting *Heliotrope Bouquet* he rescued two themes of the Creole's artistry (A and B) and added, like a farewell, two of his own (C and D) to complete the rag form.

The fireworks, literal and figurative, of the Louisiana Purchase Exposition (St. Louis World's Fair) of 1904 highlighted the classic ragtime era and floodlighted some famous public ragtime contests. The fair is celebrated in two rags: Turpin's *St. Louis Rag* and a Joplin masterpiece, *The Cascades,* descriptive of the renowned Exposition water course.

From the Joplin-Turpin era is the altogether lovely and infectious country ragtime of a blind White ragtimer whom Joplin and Turpin may never have met, although he had settled in St. Louis in 1902. Charles H. Hunter, from Tennessee, died before the age of 30, like Chauvin a youthful victim of the sordid night life of the time. Hunter's sparse but precious life work is well represented here, from the 1899 *Tickled to Death* to the 1905 *Back to Life,* over-hopefully titled following a near-fatal illness but actually a prelude to his imminent death. The Hunter rags are definitive of the term "Missouri Valley country ragtime."

James Scott, one of the great trio of classicists, met Scott Joplin briefly as Scott was moving to Kansas City. Scott is the Liszt to the Chopin in Joplin—brilliant and often bravura, melodic, taxingly technical, but—unlike Joplin—unshadowed. His work—uniformly high-level—is generously represented here by rags from the 1906 *Frog Legs* to the late-period *Don't Jazz Me Rag—I'm Music* of 1921.

Kansas City also harbored the financially successful (and melodically gifted) White composer and publisher Charles L. Johnson, who wrote prolifically under several names (including Raymond Birch). Capable of potboilers, Johnson was also capable of near-classic rags too (e.g. *"Blue Goose," Cum Bac Rag*).

Elsewhere in ragtime-fertile Missouri, another White ragtimer, Percy Wenrich, wrote ragtime both original and cognizant of ragtime's Black sources, as for example *Ashy Africa.* Beyond the rag genre, Wenrich has earned immortality for non-pop pop songs that have become in effect American folk songs over the years; one need only mention *Put on Your Old Grey Bonnet*—and there were others.

And, from Carthage, was a brilliant White pianist, Clarence Woods, a nickelodeon silent-movie avatar of limited but irreplaceably personal published output. Like many now-forgotten talents of his day, Woods stressed performance over composing in an art that embraced both. He is well represented here by his *Slippery Elm* (1912) and *Sleepy Hollow* (1918).

As Scott Joplin left the St. Louis ragtime stage, its last-scene figures were entering: Rob Hampton (*Cataract Rag* and *Agitation Rag*) and Charles Thompson (*The Lily*). Like the earlier patriarchal Turpin, Thompson was a saloon keeper, but in *his* latter days—*o tempora o mores!*—a juke box stood where once the piano had been.

Joplin's later years in New York included his meeting a young White would-be ragtime composer and his offering the same hand of friend and master that he had earlier extended to Hayden and Marshall in Sedalia and to Chauvin and (briefly but decisively) James Scott in St. Louis. The New York protegé, Joseph Francis Lamb, was 20 when he met Joplin in 1907. He had previously published schoolboy pop efforts. He played his initial ragtime essay, *Sensation,* for Joplin. Sensing talent—perhaps even genius—the famous Black composer helped with its arrangement and publication.

His faith was amply justified. Joe Lamb went on to become one of ragtime's immortal three (and the only White member of the *troika*), one who developed a very personal sensitivity into the most haunting chromatic harmonies and exquisitely Chopinesque *morbidezza* in all ragtime literature. It is impossible to conceive of the classic Missouri Valley Black ragtime without its rounding out in the work of this White Eastern genius. It is rightly represented here with six piano rags from the initial and highly Negroid *Sensation* of 1908 to the authentic Lamb classicism of *Ragtime Nightingale* and *Reindeer* of 1915.

Playing a Lamb rag is an object lesson in the interpretive possibilities of classic piano ragtime, possibilities that were implicit in the form from Joplin on, but were generally ignored until today. The opportunity—and need—for *rubato* (which is to say: judicious, expressive variations in tempo, especially within the measure) have traditionally been avoided by ragtime performers. And yet a page from Lamb or the mature Joplin (like a page from Chopin) seems to cry out for the quickening of a pulse here and the tender prolonging of a phrase there. In the ragtime era proper, the music was used (like the minuet originally) to accompany dancing, hence the inflexible tempo. This became a habit while at the same time—to compensate for that rigidity—ragtime playing underwent a speeding up to ruinous tempos (see Joplin's warnings on nearly every rag).

Only very recently, as classically trained and oriented players have begun (70 years later!) to play what once they had scorned, are freer, more flexible and more expressive modes of performance replacing the old, racing, pounding honky-tonk beat. Now, at last—the clichés destroyed—individual feeling and taste can reign. Ragtime can now be *interpreted,* and sensitive players (without losing the intoxicating syncopations and metric denials) find Joplin, Scott and Lamb responsive to the caressing hand.

This present collection might have been titled *A Ragtime Repertory,* for many a full concert of American ragtime of the classic era can be programmed from it—or, even, a program series, spanning time, from the fruitful early nexus with folk song and folk dance on to the true native classicism, Black and White, of the Big Three. The attempt here has been to let a time and a place speak for itself, without categories, in a music that is the timeless voice of an era and the universal *genius loci* of a local area. Or, to change the symbolism: here is a mother lode of gold in our American heritage, now at last—in our Bicentennial decade—being rediscovered.

RUDI BLESH

New York
June, 1973

Contents

Scott Joplin with others

Joe Jordan

Joseph F. Lamb

Arthur Marshall

Artie Matthews

James Scott

Cataract.

RAG.

ROBERT HAMPTON.

Mod.-Slow.

1

Agitation Rag.

ROBERT HAMPTON.
Composer of Cataract Rag.

5

Tickled to Death.

CHAS HUNTER.

Tempo di Rag.

TRIO.

POSSUM AND TATERS.

CHAS. HUNTER,
Composer of "Queen of Love," two-step, and
"A Tennessee Tantalizer," a rag-time tickler.

Tempo di Rag.

Back to Life.

By CHAS. HUNTER.
Composer of TICKLED TO DEATH.

Dedicated to CHARLES M. SMITH of Chicago

Cum Bac
Rag

CHAS. L. JOHNSON

Piano

TRIO

"BLUE GOOSE"
RAG

RAYMOND BIRCH
Composer of "Powder Rag"

MAPLE LEAF RAG.

BY SCOTT JOPLIN.

Tempo di marcia.

ORIGINAL RAGS.

Picked by
SCOTT JOPLIN.

Arranged by
CHAS. N. DANIELS.

31

"THE EASY WINNERS"

A RAG TIME TWO STEP.

By SCOTT JOPLIN.

Introduction.

Not fast.

A BREEZE FROM ALABAMA.

MARCH AND TWO-STEP.

SCOTT JOPLIN.

Not fast.

ELITE SYNCOPATIONS.

Not fast.

By SCOTT JOPLIN.

Dedicated to James Brown and his Mandolin Club.

THE ENTERTAINER.

A RAG TIME TWO STEP.

INTRO:

Not fast.

BY SCOTT JOPLIN.

PALM LEAF RAG

SCOTT JOPLIN
Composer of "Maple Leaf Rag"

Play a little slow

THE CASCADES.

A RAG.

SCOTT JOPLIN.
Composer of "Maple Leaf Rag."

Tempo di Marcia.

THE CHRYSANTHEMUM.

An Afro-American Intermezzo.

By SCOTT JOPLIN.
Composer of "Maple Leaf Rag."

Slow March Tempo.

"PLEASANT MOMENTS"

Ragtime Waltz

By SCOTT JOPLIN
Composer of "Maple Leaf Rag"

Reflection Rag
(SYNCOPATED MUSINGS)

SCOTT JOPLIN

Slow March Tempo.

"SWIPESY"

CAKE WALK.

By SCOTT JOPLIN
and
ARTHUR MARSHALL.

SUN FLOWER SLOW DRAG.

RAG TIME TWO STEP.

By SCOTT JOPLIN
and
SCOTT HAYDEN.

INTRO.
Not fast.

"Something Doing."

A RAGTIME TWO STEP.

SCOTT JOPLIN.
SCOTT HAYDEN.

Intro.
Not fast.

HELIOTROPE BOUQUET
A Slow Drag Two Step.

N.B. Do not play this piece fast. It is never right to play "Ragtime" fast. Composers.

By SCOTT JOPLIN
and LOUIS CHAUVIN.

NAPPY LEE.

(A Slow Drag.)

JOE JORDAN

INTRO.
Not too fast.

SENSATION.

A Rag.

JOSEPH F. LAMB.
Arr by Scott Joplin.

Tempo di marcia.

ETHIOPIA RAG.

By JOSEPH F. LAMB.

Slow March Tempo. ♩ = 100.

American Beauty.

JOSEPH F. LAMB.

Ragtime Nightingale.

JOSEPH F. LAMB.

Reindeer.
RAG TIME TWO-STEP.

JOSEPH F. LAMB.

TRIO.

mp-f legato.

Bohemia
RAG

JOSEPH F. LAMB

TRIO

mp legato

mf

cresc.

r.h.

l.h.

ff

fz

"Kinklets"
TWO STEP

By ARTHUR MARSHALL.
Composer of "Swipesy" Cake Walk.

Introd. Moderato.

Two Step

THE PEACH.

A Sentimental Rag.

By ARTHUR MARSHALL.

Play slow.

Pastime Rag.
(A Slow Drag.)

No. 1.

ARTIE MATTHEWS.

Mod. Not Fast.

Dont Fake.

TRIO.

Pastime Rag.

A SLOW DRAG.

ARTIE MATTHEWS.

No. 2.

Pastime Rag

A SLOW DRAG

No. 3.

ARTIE MATTHEWS

Pastime Rag
A SLOW DRAG

No. 4.

Moderato *Don't fake*

ARTIE MATTHEWS

129

Pastime Rag
No. 5.

ARTIE MATTHEWS

Frog Legs Rag.

JAMES SCOTT.

Dedicated to Mr. and Mrs. Mett. Penn. K. C. Mo.

Kansas City Rag.

JAMES SCOTT.
Composer of " Frog Legs."

Not too fast.

Great Scott Rag

JAMES SCOTT.
Comp. of "Frog Legs Rag."

Not fast.

HILARITY RAG.

JAMES SCOTT.
Comp."Frog Legs."

Evergreen Rag.

JAMES SCOTT.

TRIO.

New Era Rag

JAS. SCOTT

Not too fast

Troubadour Rag

JAMES SCOTT

Don't Jazz Me- Rag
(I'M MUSIC)

JAMES SCOTT

Not too fast

The Lily Rag.

CHAS. THOMPSON.
Arr. by Artie Matthews.

Harlem Rag.
Two Step.

Arr. by D.S. De Lisle.

TOM TURPIN.

162   Tom Turpin

THE ST. LOUIS RAG.

By TOM TURPIN.

ASHY AFRICA

AN AFRICAN RAG

PERCY WENRICH

TRIO

To my friend Phil Epstein

Slippery Elm Rag

CLARENCE WOODS

SLEEPY HOLLOW RAG

(UNIQUE RAG NOVELTY)

By CLARENCE WOODS

Composer of "GRAVEYARD BLUES"

NOTE: *This number is a decided novelty and should be played SLOW and SOFT. Particular attention should be paid to the sustainet notes and tremolos. They can be made to "stand out" without forcing them.* CLARENCE WOODS, *the composer.*

* *This number can be played for anything except a waltz by slightly altering the style and tempo as illustration. This illustration also gives an example of a simplified movement for measurues containing tremolo effect.*

Copyright *MCMXVIII by Will L. Livernash*
Kansas City, Mo.

Index of Titles